LEONARDO DA VINCI

THE LIFE & TIMES OF

Leonardo Da Vinci

BY
James Brown

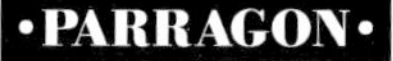

This edition first published by
Parragon Book Service Ltd in 1996

Parragon Book Service Ltd
Unit 13–17 Avonbridge Trading Estate
Atlantic Road, Avonmouth
Bristol BS11 9QD

Produced by Magpie Books,
an imprint of Robinson Publishing

Illustrations courtesy of Bridgeman Art Library

ISBN 0 75251 587 X

A copy of the British Library Cataloguing in Publication Data is available from the British Library.

Typeset by Whitelaw & Palmer Ltd, Glasgow
Printed in Singapore

CHILDHOOD

Like the *Mona Lisa* (or *La Gioconda*), his most celebrated creation, Leonardo eludes us. It is not simply his distance in time that makes him hard to make out. Others of his period, such as his young rival, Michelangelo, or Cesare Borgia who employed him for a time, had personalities which time has done little to dim. Nor is it simply lack of material: though not all of Leonardo's notebooks have survived, what we do have represents an unrivalled record of an individual's thoughts. However, the notebooks are the record primarily of Leonardo's intellectual life. Except in a handful of entries, he gives us nothing of the kind one might expect in a private journal. Nor does the bias of his talents define him. He has come to represent the legend of universal genius, and there is a surprising degree of truth in the legend. If one searches in his work, again he shies away. Fewer than fifteen of his paintings survive, and none of his sculptures. The accidents of history have destroyed some, but Leonardo was never prolific. Indeed, he was notorious for leaving works unfinished, and much of his fame rested on what he had conceived but left undone. This was not mere fecklessness, and nor was he a particularly slow worker. But he seldom started to create until he had seen what he sought in his mind's eye, and just as he seems elusive to us, his vision often seemed elusive to him. In an age when artists tended to establish conventional lines of work, partly to be as productive as possible, and so make a living, Leonardo felt driven to reconceive the treatment of his subjects radically with each new work. There are no easy generalizations to make about such a man.

Leonardo was an illegitimate child, born in the village of Vinci on 15 April 1452 at 10.30 p.m. Of his mother we know little, beyond the fact that she was called Caterina, and was in her early twenties. Shortly after giving birth to Leonardo, she got married to a man with the nickname Accattabriga, 'the squabbler', and moved to a neighbouring village. Possibly Leonardo's father helped her to a husband by way of providing for her. He was a notary, Piero Da Vinci. His family had followed the same profession in Florence for generations, but also owned land around Vinci. His father, Leonardo's grandfather, had broken with family tradition by not pursuing the family profession, living instead off the family's modest estate.

Ser Piero married for the first time in the year of Leonardo's birth. His bride, Albiera Amadori, was a prudent match and brought a decent dowry with her. They lived for the most part in Florence. Leonardo's mother was nearer to hand –

just over a mile away – but within two or three years of Leonardo's birth she had her own family to think about.

By 1457 the infant Leonardo was living with his grandfather, on whose tax return for that year he appears. He had most likely lived with his mother for his first months, and moved to his grandfather's when she got married. His father spent most of his time in Florence, but his upbringing was probably not loveless. Besides his grandparents, there was his uncle Francesco. When Francesco died in 1506 he left his property to his illegitimate nephew. This was unusual enough for the legitimate ones to contest the will, but Francesco's intentions were clear.

By the standards of the time, Leonardo was uneducated. It would scarcely have been possible to receive more than a basic elementary schooling in Vinci. Even if it had there would have been no point in Leonardo acquiring the Classical, humanist scholarship that was the backbone of education at the time. It was the way into the professions, but since Leonardo was illegitimate, that avenue was closed anyway. In later years he would try to remedy the deficiency by acquiring Latin, but perhaps it was as well that he avoided conventional lessons, for they might have tied clogs to his roving mind.

In later years Leonardo recorded a childhood memory on the back of a page of notes. He was investigating the flight of birds in the hope of emulating them, making close observations of a kite, and it reminded him of a dream: 'Writing about the kite seems to be my destiny since among the first recollections of my infancy it seemed to me that as I was in my cradle a kite came to me and opened my mouth with its tail and struck me several times with its tail inside my lips.' Freud makes much of this in an essay on Leonardo, though unfortunately he mistranslates the word for kite as 'vulture'. Even so, it is a suggestive passage. At a time when one might suppose the infant sought only his mother's breast, Leonardo substitutes a powerful bird of prey – perhaps an image both of aspiration to soar beyond the common bounds, and of dammed-up aggression.

During the late 1460s his circumstances changed. His grandfather died; his grandmother did not long survive him; his uncle married. He moved to Florence.

APPRENTICESHIP

Leonardo's father seems to have decided that he ought to become an artist, and apprenticed him to a master-artist of his acquaintance, Verrocchio. There is a story from Leonardo's youth that may explain why Ser Piero decided his son's future as he did. A tenant of Ser Piero's had found a piece of wood, which caught his fancy, and asked Ser Piero to take it to Florence to have a design painted on it to make it into a shield. Piero decided his son could do it – perhaps because he had already spotted Leonardo's talent, or just as likely, since Piero was a good bourgeois, because it would be cheap. He gave Leonardo the twisted root, and told him to do what he could with it. Leonardo had it straightened out with heat and pressure, and prepared the surface with a mixture of his own devising. Then he sought inspiration. He decided to paint a Medusa's head. He gathered lizards and snakes, grasshoppers and bats, and the like. He killed and dismembered them. Out of the pieces he arranged the most hideous still life – or rather still death – he could conceive. Then he painted it. The stench in his little room was stomach-turning, but Leonardo paid no attention. Eventually he completed the work and sent for his father. Before he let his father in, he arranged the room, setting the Medusa's head on a stand opposite the door, and blocking out the sunlight, save for a single beam that picked out his work. When Ser Piero entered he had the shock of his life. However, he soon recovered himself. He took his son's work and sold it to a merchant for a hundred ducats, and bought his tenant an ordinary shield. Ser Piero was not perhaps quite as astute as he thought: the merchant sold Leonardo's shield on to the Duke of Milan for three hundred ducats.

It's pleasant to imagine that this incident might have planted the idea in Ser Piero's head that his son should become an artist, and led him to apprentice the boy to

Andrea del Verrocchio in Florence, but really there were few options for the bastard son of a bourgeois. Bastard sons of popes and dukes fared well enough in the Renaissance, but not those of notaries. However, the story does point to one of the defining features of Leonardo's talent: his combination of minute observation of nature with a powerful, and sometimes fantastic, imagination.

The business which Leonardo was set to learn was overall unlike any modern equivalent. Apprenticeship in a *bottega* or workshop was not like going to art school today, and still less like becoming a student at a famous artist's studio in the last century. Leonardo was an apprentice, not a student; he aimed to become a master-craftsman, not an artist in the Romantic sense of the word. There was little of our sense of works being the unique product of an individual vision, which accordingly required the artist's involvement at every stage of their execution. Verrocchio was a designer and technician as much as an artist. He would decorate furniture and china, and make a host of items for interior decor as requested. He would also cheerfully let the abler apprentices do some of the work, whether that was mixing paints and dyes, preparing canvases, or, as in Leonardo's case, painting angels. Leonardo would challenge some of these assumptions in the course of his career, but not all.

Leonardo seems to have got on well with

his master. He remained with him long after he had qualified as a master himself. Though the work could be menial for new apprentices, the atmosphere was stimulating. It was a time of rapid developments in the craft of painting, in particular to do with the discovery of perspective. This was more than a technical question. For an enquiring mind the problem of how to represent the world led naturally to the broader question of how the world was made. Leonardo would become fascinated with the way things worked, whether they were birds or people. This led to the attempt to make machines. Leonardo's interest in technology was unique in its depth and range, but the example of Verrocchio must have stimulated it. Among Verrocchio's celebrated works

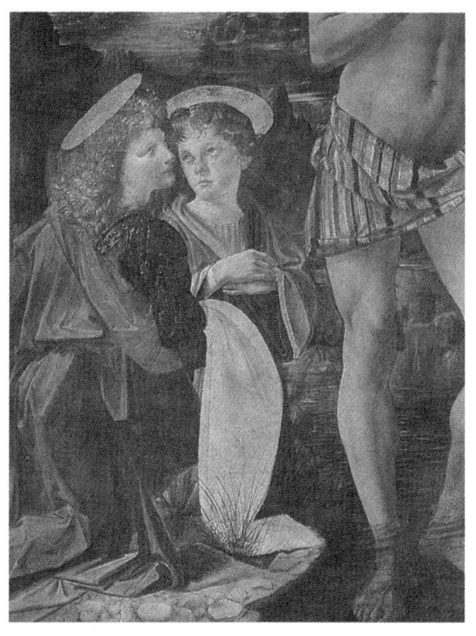

Angels from Verrocchio's *Baptism of Christ*

was the erection of a gilt ball on top of the Duomo in Florence in 1471. The Florentines were inordinately proud of this great cathedral, which had been centuries in the making, and such an addition to it was an affair of state. For Verrocchio, however, it was a matter first of design, then of engineering. He had to make a ball of a diameter of twenty feet and gild it. Then he had to raise it some 350 feet and secure it. This may sound sufficiently unimpressive today, when anyone attempting such a feat can call upon legions of specialists who can supply all the answers and some powerful machines to put them into action. In Verrocchio's day the execution of such a task entailed finding one's own solution to all the problems, and in the process one might make technological discoveries that put one in the vanguard of innovation.

Not everything in the *bottega* was quite so technical, but it was a natural place to discuss geometry, mathematics, aspects of applied chemistry, and machines as well as art and design.

In 1472 Leonardo qualified as a Master, but he remained with Verrocchio. His earliest surviving painting is work done in collaboration with the older man. Verrocchio had been commissioned by the monastery of San Salvi to paint the baptism of Christ by John the Baptist. To Leonardo he entrusted the background and one of the two angels kneeling on the left. Leonardo's landscape draws the eye. It is framed by an exotic palm-tree on the left, and by wooded crags on the right. Far into the distance a river meanders, the source of the water that the Baptist pours over Christ's head. Leonardo's landscape is at once precisely realized, and fantastic: both real and imagined. His angel combines similar qualities. It kneels to the left of its fellow, with its back to us, looking half over its shoulder at Christ. It's a difficult posture to capture, especially since the angel is enfolded in drapery, whose sensuous curves and falls Leonardo delighted in. The angel is beautiful, but, partly because it is turning away from us, also remote. When Verrocchio painted an angel, he broke with established Gothic convention far enough to seek out angelic models, but by comparison with his pupil's work, the result is earthbound, if appealing. There's a clarity about his portrayal that Leonardo shies away from – something confirmed, coincidentally, by X-rays of the picture, which have shown that Verrocchio created the clear lines of his figures by using white lead for highlighting, whereas Leonardo worked by accumulating innumerable thin layers of paint, in which shades blend imperceptibly into one another. The effect is more subtle and more elusive. It is also emotionally and spiritually more powerful. Though in the middle of the sky, above Christ, the hands of God poke out of a cloud, releasing the dove of the Holy Ghost in a blaze of light, so that its beams mingle with the water St John pours over Christ, a more profound insight into the divine is offered by Leonardo's angel. It seems real, in the sense of not being merely stylized or conventional. Yet it is otherworldly, as it looks back to Christ with an expression somewhere between admiration, pity and incomprehension of the mortal life he has chosen to embrace. Only an immortal could look quite like that.

Vasari, Leonardo's earliest biographer, says that when Verrocchio saw how his pupil painted angels, he forswore them. It seems that Leonardo must have become his master's junior partner until in 1481 or 1482 he moved to Milan.

FLORENCE

The world in which Leonardo spent his early adulthood and created his first works embraced beauty and violence. Florence was an independent power, a city-state, one of several that made up much of Renaissance Italy. They feuded and allied with each other, and were fought over by the great powers of the day, principally Spain and France. Florence was also the home of Leonardo's younger contemporary,

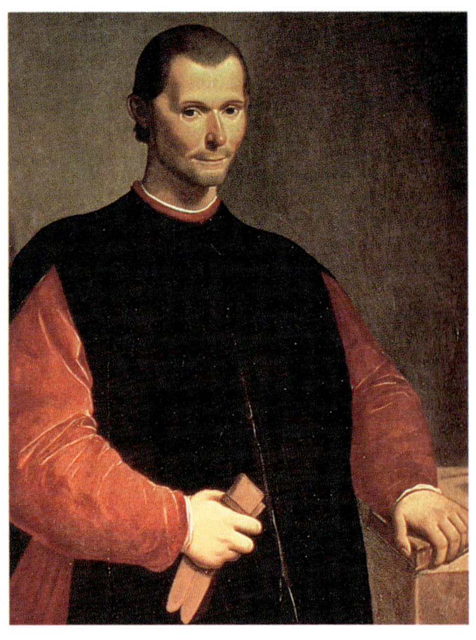

Machiavelli by Santi di Tito

Niccolo Machiavelli, whose political thought, especially in *The Prince*, reflects the unprincipled power-play of this world, but also its quest for glory and fulfilment.

It was a republic, at least in name. Its leading family, the Medici, enjoyed quasi-royal status. The head of the family in Leonardo's day was Lorenzo the Magnificent. He was the most powerful man in Florence, but had no official position. At the age of twenty he had assumed power. A cultured man, like many dukes of other city-states, he patronized the arts in part to maintain his position. But he was also something of a collector, and played the lute and composed songs as well. It was he who made the gesture of having the bones of the medieval poet Dante, one of Florence's most famous sons, brought back to Florence. He also favoured the living.

The Florence over which he presided afforded a life of luxury to the privileged. The monk Savonarola would later condemn them for their decadence. Yet there remained a procedure that was meant to ensure probity, and Leonardo fell victim to it. Throughout the city were placed open drums, into which anonymous accusations could be dropped. On 8 April 1476 some unknown hand deposited a note accusing four young men of committing sodomy with one Jacopo Saltarelli: 'the said Jacopo, having suffered many misfortunes, complies with the wicked pleasures of certain persons. He

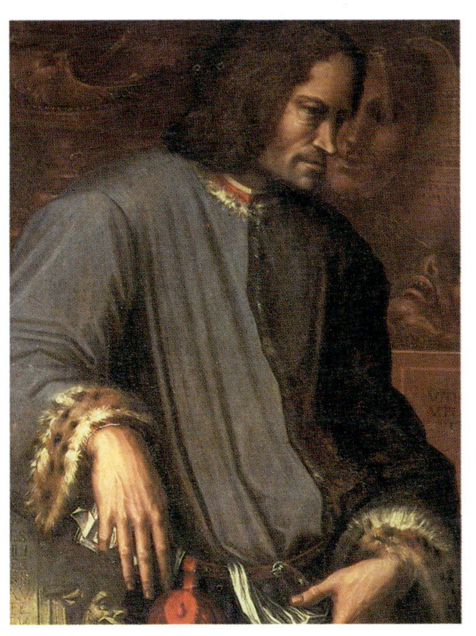

Lorenzo the Magnificent by Giorgio Vasari

has come to do many things – that is to serve several dozen people . . .' Leonardo was one of the four accused. He was a flamboyant dresser, and a notably beautiful young man – perhaps his appearance had attracted the malice of his accuser. The accusations were thrown out, with the proviso that should further evidence come to light they could be revived. However, the legal process took time, and before the verdict was reached Leonardo had an anxious time. Though homosexual behaviour was enjoying something of a vogue, and accusations were seldom successful, sodomy remained a capital offence. A man such as Leonardo, without connections, would be more vulnerable than at least one of his fellow-accused, whose family was connected with the Medici. At one point Leonardo addressed a petition to the head of one of the city's guilds, in which he sought assistance, pointing out, 'You know, as I have told you before, that I am without any friends.' On the other side of the same sheet is a note that possibly dates from this period: 'If there is no love, what then?' It seems to speak of betrayal and disillusion.

By the end of the 1470s Leonardo had begun to make his way as an artist, but he was hardly well known. The first commission he is known to have been given as an individual occurs in 1478. He was to produce a picture for the altar of the chapel of St Bernard in the Signoria. He never finished it. At some point in 1478 he must have been given work, since one note for that year records '1478 I began the two Madonnas.'

In the same year he witnessed the full severity of the law. The Medici were mighty, but their power was not uncontested. Florence was riven by factionalism, which periodically exploded in blood. One such Leonardo would have heard of shortly after arriving: in 1470 opponents of the Medici tried to take Prato, a town under Florentine control. The young Lorenzo had had the ringleaders executed, and pardoned the others. Another such outburst occurred on 26 April 1478. It was a Sunday. Lorenzo and his brother were in the Duomo when the conspirators struck. His brother Giuliano perished; Lorenzo escaped with a wound. The assassination had been intended to rouse the city to liberate itself; instead it rallied Medici loyalists, who scoured the town for the plotters. Soon bodies were being strung up and hacked about – that was before a hundred-odd death sentences were handed down. Leonardo says very little of politics in his copious notes, but certainly noticed something of this failed coup. When one of the conspirators, Bernardo di Bandino Baroncelli, was snatched by the long arm of the Medici from Constantinople, whither he had fled, Leonardo made a sketch of him as he dangled from the rope on 29 December 1479, coolly noting details of the colour of his clothes in the corner.

By then he seems no longer to have been lodging with Verrocchio. It's possible to assign several other works to this first period of his independence. There was a design for a tapestry showing Adam and

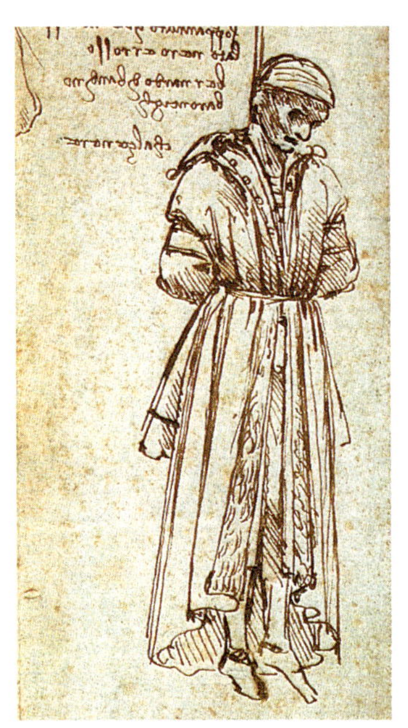

Leonardo's sketch of the hanged man, Bernardo di Bandino Baroncelli

Eve, which, like so many of Leonardo's conceptions, was never completed. Then there was the portrait of Ginevra de' Benci, with its strangely ominous feeling, as the face merges with the shadows of the spiky juniper bushes, and seems to block our way to the characteristically appealing Leonardo landscape that can just be glimpsed beyond her. As ever with Leonardo, the picture thrives on the uncertainty it conjures in one's mind. Where do its separate elements begin and end? Why does it make one feel so uneasy? If *Ginevra de' Benci* works upon the viewer largely by what is concealed, *Saint Jerome* proceeds by the extreme clarity with which Leonardo represents the saint's suffering and ageing body. He is beating himself with a stone, kneeling in front of the lion, whose friendship, so the legend has it, he won by pulling a thorn from its paw. However, Leonardo's lion looks anything but amiable: it roars as the saint aims another blow at himself. Jerome ignores the creature, his face turned upwards to heaven. So effectively has he mortified the flesh that he seems half dead already. Though unfinished, it's another disturbing image.

Considering the atmosphere of the work he was producing, it is not surprising that Leonardo seems to have been unhappy. Perhaps he felt something of the depression that occasionally overcomes gifted and introspective people, when they sense talents within themselves which they cannot find the way to use. Any feeling of disproportion between his inner sense of himself and

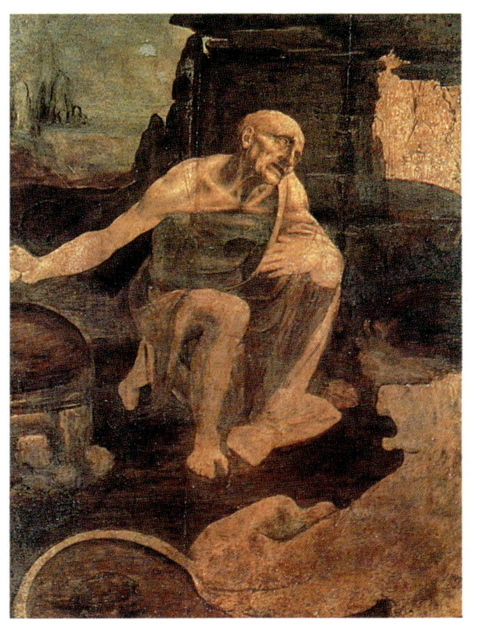

Saint Jerome

the figure he cut in Florence must have been exacerbated by the circumstances of his birth, which impaired his social standing. He must have seen his father often, for Florence was quite compact. This may have reminded him of the way in which his parents had, if not quite deserted him, then at least failed to love and care for him as they did their respective legitimate children. His personal life may also have emphasized his want of status. On one page of his notes someone else has written, 'Leonardo, my Leonardo, why such torment?', followed by something about love. Apparently in response, Leonardo then wrote, 'Do not despise me, for I am not poor. That man is poor who has great desires. Where shall I put myself? You shall know soon.'

Possibly this was the business that drove him to leave Florence. If he did indeed crave prestige, then his omission from a select band of Florentine artists sent by Lorenzo to Rome to work for the Pope must have stung him. Verrocchio had already left Florence to work on an equestrian statue in Venice, and had presumably not asked Leonardo to go with him. He seems to have been left desperate for work, for in March 1481 he made an agreement with the monastery of San Donato to paint the *Adoration of the Magi*. The penalties for failure to complete the work were uncommonly harsh, and included the provision of a dowry for the daughter of a man who had left them an estate. If he succeeded, a third of the estate would be his, but he wouldn't be allowed to sell it for three years, in case the monks

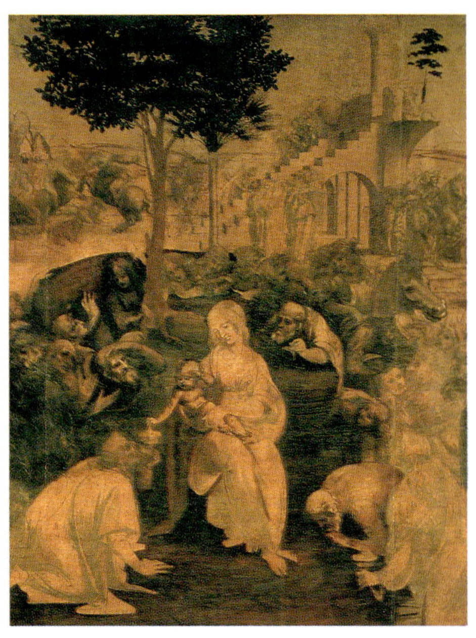

Adoration of the Magi

wanted to buy it back. Leonardo started the work; he made sketches, and prepared the monochrome for the picture itself. It shows the Madonna as an island of enchanted tranquillity in a stormy sea of passionate faces and bodies in all manner of postures. The monks tried to chivvy and encourage him. They sent him a bushel of wheat, and then in September they sent a cask of wine to his house. That is the last definite record of Leonardo's presence in Florence for several years. Shortly afterwards he abandoned the monks and his groundbreaking picture of the Adoration.

MILAN AND IL MORO

Leonardo decided to make a new life in Milan. With all his other accomplishments he was also a talented musician, and according to Vasari he had persuaded Lorenzo the Magnificent to recommend him to Ludovico Sforza as a player. He seems to have travelled to Milan with Atalante Migliorotti, who was a musician, and brought an unusual lute, wrought in silver in the shape of a horse's head, which he had made as a present for

Ludovico. He had many other things on his mind besides music, however. He wrote, either *en route* or perhaps shortly after arriving, an odd letter to Ludovico, advertising his many talents. He lists the various feats he can perform. He concentrates on his abilities as a military engineer, promising Ludovico movable bridges, versatile water defences, extra-powerful mortars, underground secret passages, and what sounds like a very early tank: 'I will make covered cars, safe and unassailable, which will enter among the enemy with their artillery, and there is no company of men-at-arms so great that they will not break it. And behind these the infantry will be able to follow quite unharmed and without any hindrance.' Having proffered this array of technological weaponry, almost as an afterthought he mentions his abilities in architecture, water supply, sculpture and painting. The position of these comments does not, however, betoken modest estimate of his artistic talent, for he says, 'I can do in painting whatever can be done, as well as any other, be he who may.' As a parting shot Leonardo adds that he could also make a statue of a horse to commemorate Ludovico's father, Francesco Sforza, Duke of Milan. One would love to know whether this bizarre self-advertisement was ever sent. Whether it was or not, it suggests someone who had been thwarted in his ambitions as an artist, and is determined boldly to turn his daydreams to good account by amazing the world and offering it what it wants. After all, rulers in Renaissance Italy were always fighting, if

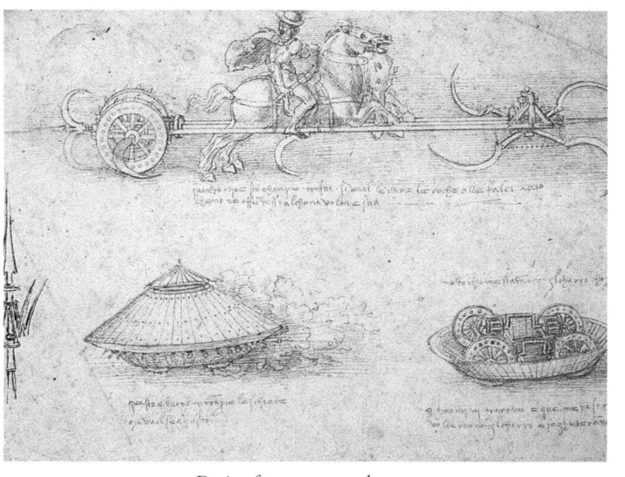

Design for an armoured car

not someone else, then each other. The world may have slighted his talents as a painter, but he would show them that he could do what no mere painter could even dream of – and, what's more, he was a better painter than any of them. If this is the implication of the letter, then the crowning irony is that Leonardo was quite right.

It is possible that the real purpose of the letter was contained in its penultimate paragraph, where he offers to make an equestrian statue. This project had been mooted for some time. It was a matter of the greatest importance to Ludovico, since his dynasty, the Sforzas, was of recent date. The family fortunes had been founded by his father, a *condottiere*, and an internationally celebrated work of art devoted to the glory of the Sforzas would be a political asset, not least in Milan itself, where Ludovico felt the need to shore up his position. Not only had the Sforzas ousted the Visconti dynasty to take the city, but Ludovico had all but usurped his nephew, Gian Galeazzo, the Duke of Milan. Ludovico, Il Moro ('the Moor' on account of his dark colouring), was merely the Duke of Bari.

Leonardo's choice of adopted home was astute, in that Milan boasted few artists, and was prepared to make much of any she could win from other cities. However, his career did not take off all at once. We hear of him collaborating with the Predi brothers in a contract dated April 1483 for the painting of an altarpiece in several panels for the Confraternity of the Immaculate Conception of the Blessed Virgin Mary. Leonardo was entrusted with the central panel. The Confraternity, treating him like a master-craftsman, specified their requirements as to subject, pose, richness of garments, and gold leaf, especially in the haloes. Leonardo signed the contract, and set about providing something completely different. *The Virgin of the Rocks* (confusingly, it exists in two versions – my comments relate to that in the Louvre) is as far from the conventional treatment of the Madonna that the Confraternity wanted as one could well get. For one thing, as the title indicates, Leonardo has filled the panel with rocks – not just beneath the Holy Family, but suspended above them as

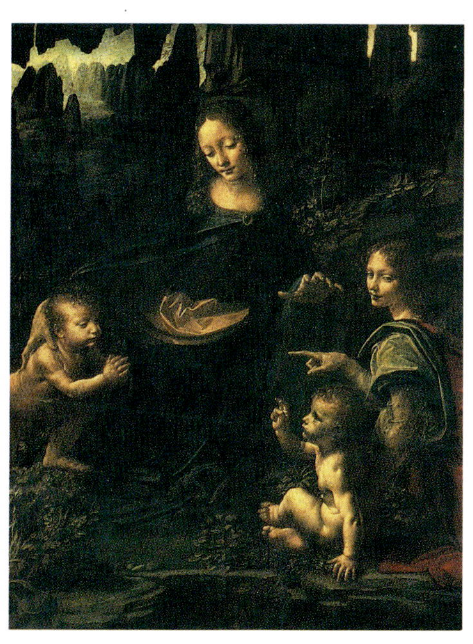

Virgin of the Rocks

well, creating a feeling of brooding weight. Yet it is not completely oppressive. The background has that characteristically appealing touch of the exotic, and the rocks do not close over the figures in the foreground in a solid mass: between them and above one can glimpse the sky. The figures themselves are gathered by a pool. At the centre is the Madonna; to one side is an infant Christ with an angel, and to the other an infant John the Baptist. Their gestures and expressions excite, without immediately gratifying, one's curiosity. The Madonna's right hand rests on the Baptist's shoulder – the gesture seems maternal, especially if one looks at the serenity of her face, but the hand is tensed, perhaps as if she has just forced the child down into a kneeling position.

He is kneeling and beseeching Christ, who sits on the other side apparently making the sign of the cross. Suddenly one glimpses one reason for the ominous beauty of the picture: the infant Christ may already anticipate his own crucifixion. But his is not the only gesture being made on that side of the picture. Immediately above his hand, the angel is pointing to St John, though her eyes seem to be focused at some point in front of the picture, just beyond the infant Christ. The Virgin's left hand hovers in the air immediately above her child's head, in a gesture that may be protective, but again there is just enough tension in the hand to make one wonder whether the intention is wholly benign.

Leonardo seems to have been incapable of

painting in the conventional, expected manner. But he did want to advance his career. Early in his time in Milan he made the astute move of painting Ludovico's young mistress, Cecilia Gallerani. She had established a semi-official position for herself by ousting all her rivals. It seems likely that her portrait is the picture now known as *Lady with an Ermine*. The ermine was one of Ludovico's many emblems, though the use to which Leonardo puts it is more complex and elusive. As one gazes at the picture, it begins to seem that there must be some subtle relationship between the qualities of the woman and the qualities of the animal she is holding. One can even start to wonder which of the two is the real subject: is the ermine there to complement the woman, or is she there merely to hold the ermine?

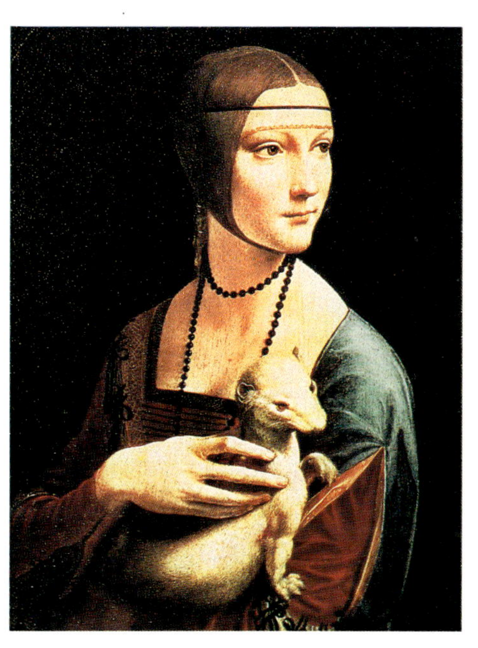

Lady with an Ermine

The cathedral of Milan had been started centuries before, and it was agreed that it needed to be crowned by an architectural feat. A competition was held, and Leonardo submitted designs. The authorities paid a carpenter to make a model based on them in July 1487, and paid Leonardo various sums over the following months. Leonardo had turned himself into an entirely plausible architect. One may wonder when and how he had made the necessary studies of building and mechanics, but his work makes it clear that he had. In the event the competition was judged to be a draw, and on 13 April 1490 it was decided to combine all the models. Leonardo seems eventually to have withdrawn from the project.

In all likelihood Leonardo no longer cared. He had more prestigious projects in hand than a share in the design of part of a cathedral. He had secured the contract for the equestrian statue that he seems to have been angling for in the letter to Ludovico. He was almost Ludovico's court artist, dealing with any artistic or architectural matters the Duke cared to consult him about. His intellectual life was one of almost unexampled variety and vigour, and tirelessly he accumulated notes on a score or so of subjects. A note he wrote to himself in 1489 captures something of the extraordinary range of his interests, and the way in which he maintained them all at once. He reminds himself, among other things, to make a map of Milan and buy a book about the city and its churches, to consult various acquaintances and books about geometry and algebra, to find out about astronomy, in particular the measurement of the sun, to ask someone else about 'how people go on the ice in Flanders' and about the 'measurement of the canal, locks, and supports, and large boats; and the expense', and to consult others about waterworks. He was also pursuing work in optics, and designing inventions based on his discoveries.

On 13 January 1490 he pulled off a feat that made his name and won him favour. He designed a grand entertainment for Ludovico, The Masque of the Planets. It was on astrological themes, with a text by one Bernardo Bellincioni. But it was Leonardo's exotic designs and breathtaking special effects that attracted the most attention.

The following March found him at work as an architect, building a pavilion in the garden of the Duchess of Milan. In April he mentions at the beginning of a notebook that he had started afresh on the horse – the great statue with which Ludovico planned to amaze the world.

Three months later he welcomed a ten-year-old boy into his household. He was called Giacomo. From the first he was a troublemaker. He seems to have been poor, because Leonardo had to buy him clothes almost immediately. He lists the garments, and adds that 'when I put aside money to pay for these things he stole it from the wallet, and it was never possible to make him confess, although I was quite certain of it . . . lire 4.' Further misdemeanours followed. Giacomo came to be known as 'Salai', which means 'limb of Satan'. He remained with Leonardo until (or almost until) the artist's death. Vasari records that Salai was of uncommon grace and beauty. The boy seems to have gained a firm emotional hold on his guardian. On one page of his notes in later years Leonardo pleads, 'Salai, I want to make peace with you, not war. No more war, I give in.'

Meanwhile Leonardo continued to work. He was accumulating studies for the great statue, seeking out real horses and finding out what was technically possible. Finally he finished a model in clay. It was the same size as the finished bronze was to be – in other words, huge. The horse alone was 23 feet tall. To this were to be added the rider and the plinth. It possibly went on display in November 1493 to coincide with the betrothal of Ludovico's niece to the Emperor Maximilian. It became famous almost immediately.

The statue was never cast. Possibly it was beyond even Leonardo's technical ingenuity to make so vast a piece. However, he did make elaborate plans, which were finally scotched when Ludovico had to divert the bronze for the statue to the casting of cannon in November 1494.

During the 1490s Leonardo's household grew. As a Master he had pupils living under his roof, and servants. The name of one member of his household has excited speculation. In a notebook Leonardo recorded, 'Caterina came, 16 July 1493.' Could this have been his mother? It is impossible to know. He records money given to her in January 1494, and then some time later records Caterina's funeral expenses without further comment. Could this be a son's farewell to his mother? Leonardo's likely feelings about his parents, and his own temperament, make it just conceivable, but no more.

In 1495 he was commissioned to paint a mural in the refectory of the friary of Santa Maria delle Grazie. The friary was supported by Ludovico, so it seems likely that he gave Leonardo the commission. Leonardo decided, or perhaps was asked, to paint *The Last Supper*. It is an appropriate subject for a dining room. Leonardo so contrived it that his picture of Christ and the Apostles appeared to be a continuation of the room, so that to the monks it would seem as if Christ were eating with them. *The Last Supper* has not aged well; however, one can still glean from it some sense of Leonardo's talent for characterization. The figures are all busily and variously engaged, and it is known that Leonardo took his time in planning their arrangement and in seeking out suitable models for each of them. He used to keep a sketch book with him, so that if he saw an interesting face, he could make a record of it. It was said that sometimes he would follow people whose faces he wished to draw for hours, watching their expressions and memorizing their features, so that he

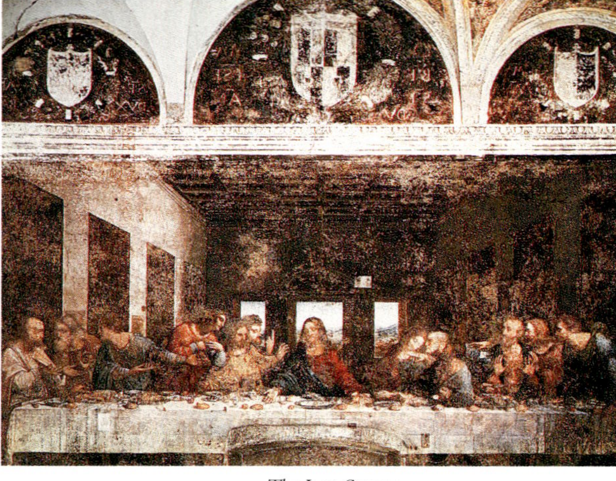

The Last Supper

could then go away and draw them from memory. However, this procedure was time-consuming, and entailed considerable periods of reflection, which to the patron eager to have the work finished sometimes seemed to be neglect. One contemporary account of Leonardo at work on *The Last Supper* makes clear how bewildering his method could seem: 'Many a time I have seen Leonardo go to work early in the morning on the platform before the Last Supper; and he would stay there from sunrise till darkness, never laying down the brush, but continuing to paint without eating or drinking. Then three or four days would pass without his touching the work, yet each day he would spend several hours examining it and criticizing the figures to himself.'

The prior became so exasperated with him that he complained to Ludovico. Called to give an account of himself, Leonardo explained that he had been searching for a model for Judas, who had to appear to be a complete villain. So far he had had no luck, but if the prior chose to insist on the completion of the painting, then he could serve as the model for Judas, since he fitted the bill exactly. Ludovico was sufficiently amused to take Leonardo's side.

Leonardo had developed his private researches. He was fascinated by the idea of flying, and designed mechanisms that he hoped would carry him to the skies. In one note he prudently resolves to test one such device over a lake so that he would have a soft landing should

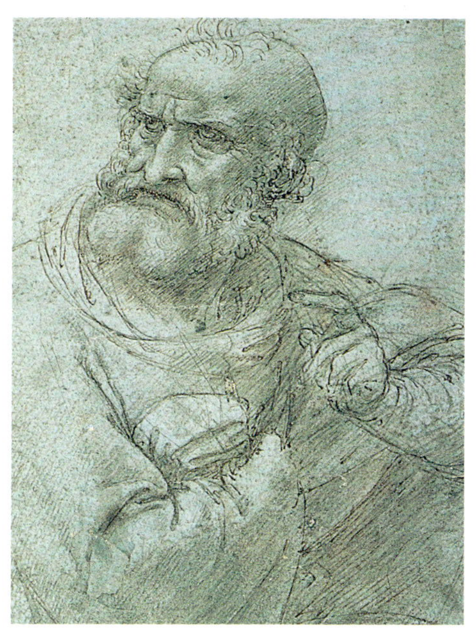

Study for an apostle for *The Last Supper*

anything go wrong. In the quest to make it possible to go where no man had gone before, he also designed a diving suit. One of the main themes in his inventions, however, is a distinctively modern one: automation. He seems to have been drawn to envisage ways of eliminating people from a host of processes. Among his designs is perhaps the first automated mass-production machine ever. It was for sharpening needles. Leonardo computed that it would be able to deal with 40,000 needles an hour, and optimistically calculated the profit that it might bring.

By the end of the 1490s the shadows were lengthening over Ludovico's Milan. He had finally succeeded to the Dukedom after the death of his nephew

– dark rumours circulated about his possible role in Gian Galeazzo's demise. Ludovico had married Beatrice d'Este, daughter of the Duke of Ferrara, for political reasons, though he had then fallen in love with his bride, but, in 1496 she died. In the violent game of international power-politics his position was growing precarious. The storm clouds were gathering. At the end of April 1499 Ludovico rewarded Leonardo with a vineyard. By the end of the summer the French had swept through Lombardy and Ludovico was on the run. The most settled period of Leonardo's life had come to an end.

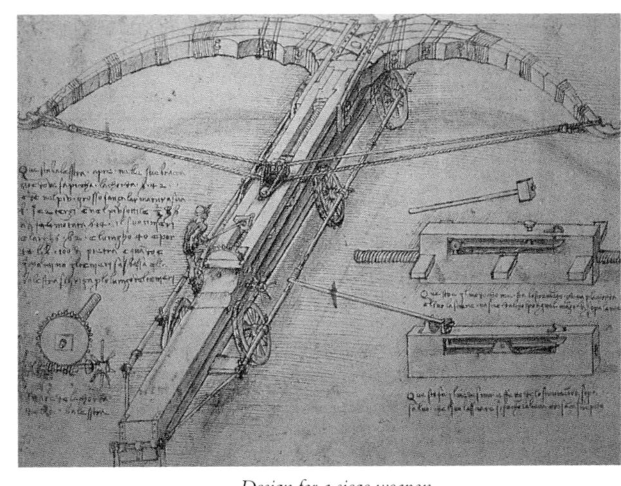

Design for a siege weapon

WANDERINGS AND REST

The French occupied the city. Leonardo packed up his things – a process partly recorded in the reminders he wrote to himself – and left. He may still have hoped that Ludovico would regain the city, and so enable him to resume his life in Milan. He'd saved a fair sum, so there was no immediate pressure to secure commissions, and he withdrew to Venice to see how the struggle for Milan ended.

He did no painting in Venice, but did pursue another strand of his work as consulting military engineer. The Venetian Senate sought his advice on how to defend their land-frontier against the Turks. Leonardo outlined a scheme to lure the Turks on to low ground, which could then be flooded, thus drowning them *en masse*. Privately, however, he expressed scruples about putting advanced military technology into the hands of wicked men. He was, perhaps, relieved when Venice came to terms with the Turks.

In April 1500 Leonardo seems to have returned to Florence. Ludovico had been captured in February, so Leonardo now had to find another patron. In the interim he agreed to do a painting for the Servite friars. He painted the *Virgin and Child*

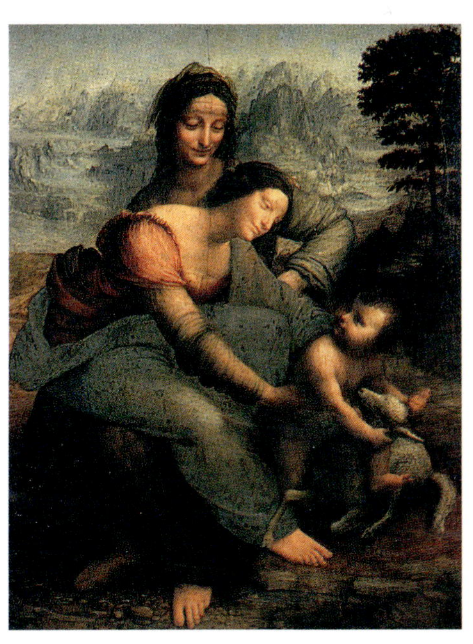

Virgin and Child with Saint Anne

with Saint Anne for them. Vasari reports that Florence was suitably impressed by the work of its now famous citizen. However, Leonardo never quite completed the picture, and finally took it to France. What there is is magnificent, but Leonardo had little patience with the mechanics of painting. Indeed, though he needed a patron, he was choosy enough to reject one who looked likely to prove too demanding. Isabella d'Este had heard much of his talents, and, priding herself on her patronage of the arts, was determined that Leonardo paint a portrait of her. Leonardo did his best to evade her.

His military consultancy in Venice may have suggested to him that the wars that had robbed him of life in Milan ought to be grasped as an opportunity, for he was now appointed military engineer to Cesare Borgia. Borgia was the son of the Pope, and in his brief, explosive and ruthless career attempted by force and guile to unite Italy. Leonardo had long designed fantastical engines of war, but he had seldom had to put them into practice. He was so enthralled by the possibility of seeing one of his schemes put into practice on the largest possible scale that he even offered his services to the Turks. It came to nothing.

By the spring of 1503 Leonardo was back in Florence, having apparently left Borgia's service. Florence at this date was seeking to revive its republican ideals. The Medici were in exile. For a time Leonardo appears to have lived on his savings, occupying himself with his many interests. For example, he pursued anatomy. At a hospital one day he interviewed an old man who claimed to be a hundred, and whose only symptom was extreme weakness. The old man died, and Leonardo promptly opened him up to find the cause of death, which appeared to be the withering of the arteries that supplied the lower body. In the same note he records making another autopsy of a two-year-old child. In an age when doctors preferred to be guided by ancient, classical texts on medicine, Leonardo's precise observations and his unrivalled capacity to record them in drawings, represented a real scientific advance. At the same time he had resumed his efforts to fly.

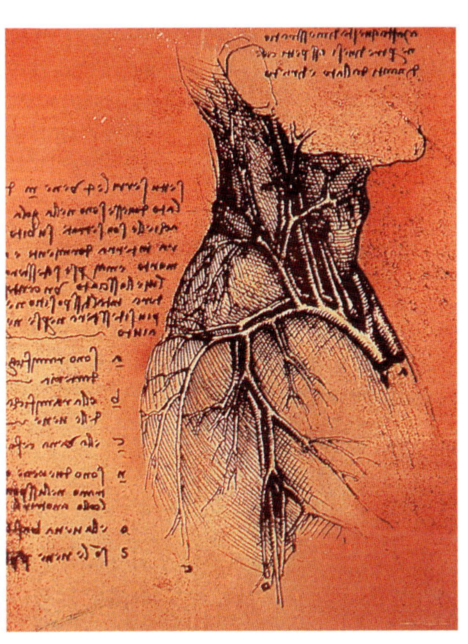

Anatomical drawing

While serving Borgia Leonardo had met Niccolò Machiavelli, who was then one of the new regime's diplomats. Machiavelli appears to have had a hand in Leonardo's employment, first in a bizarre military scheme to end a war between Florence and Pisa by means of waterworks to drown the enemy, and then as a painter. He was to paint *The Battle of Anghiari* on one wall of the Grand Council Chamber. Neither scheme was ever completed, though arguably Leonardo was on surer ground in representing war than in prosecuting it. He started work on the mural in October 1503. As ever, his preparations were meticulous; he made many sketches, and debated with himself how to select and arrange the scene. He didn't begin to apply paint until 6 June 1505. For three years he laboured on this painting, dogged

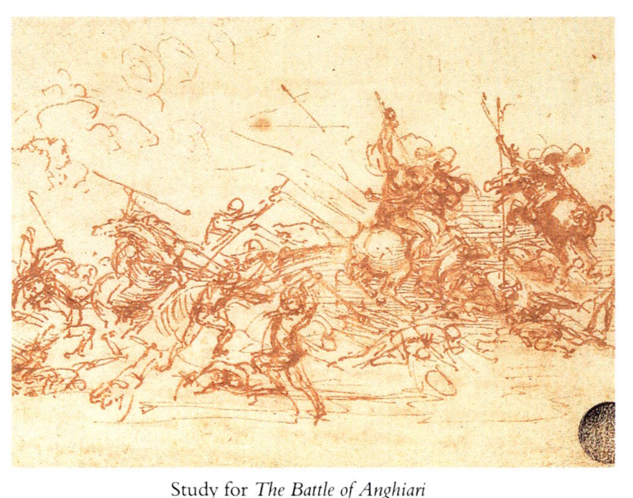

Study for *The Battle of Anghiari*

by bad luck (a freak storm damaged his cartoon) and by various technical problems. As often, he was experimenting. The usual technique for painting murals required one to work rapidly. Leonardo sought an alternative that would allow him more time, and make it possible to work with oils. But it seems to have gone wrong.

Being back in Florence, he must have met his father again. Ser Piero died in the summer of 1504. Leonardo recorded his death twice in his notebooks, but without any other outward expression of feeling. He had never felt particularly bound to Florence, and the combination of his father's death, the problems he had encountered with the painting, and the rivalry of a younger generation of artists (especially Michelangelo) made him contemplate departure. When the French expressed an interest in employing him, the chance seemed too good to miss. They were so powerful in Italy that they could oblige the Florentine authorities to set aside their contractual claims on Leonardo. He seems to have been glad to escape back to Milan, where he resumed something of the range of activities he had undertaken in the time of Ludovico. The French were flatteringly keen to retain him. Wearisome family affairs dragged him back to Florence on occasion. Ser Piero had died intestate, and his sons by his various marriages contested the estate, denying anything to Leonardo. Then his uncle Francesco died in 1506, having made Leonardo his heir. Leonardo's legitimate half-brothers went to law to get the property for themselves. Since he was in bad odour with the Florentine authorities, he feared that judgement would go against him, and therefore elicited the support of the French king, Louis XII, to support his case. The court finally vindicated him, and in the summer of 1508 he returned to Milan.

In the midst of his many activities he continued to paint. At some point in this period he painted the *Mona Lisa.* Like its creator, this most famous of his works is shrouded in mystery. Vasari tells a story that accounts for the half-smile that seems to play across her lips. According to Vasari the sitter was the wife of one Francesco del Giocondo, and 'while Leonardo was drawing her portrait he

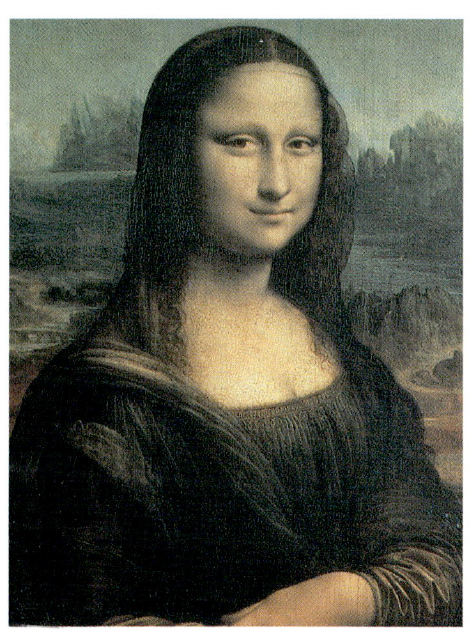

Mona Lisa

engaged people to play and sing, and jesters to keep her merry, and remove that melancholy which painting usually gives to portraits.' According to one version La Gioconda was depressed at the time by the loss of a child. If there is any truth in the story, then one has to observe that some of this melancholy remained. The painting has suffered over the years, but even in its original form the sitter was beset with shadows, both in her own sombre clothes, and among the rocks behind her.

At some point during his second period in Milan he met a young Lombard nobleman, Francesco Melzi. He was eager to learn all that Leonardo could teach, and became a permanent member of his entourage. He was younger than

Salai, and though Salai's reaction to the introduction of this rival into the household is not recorded, it seems possible that he was disgruntled.

Lombardy was still one of the most keenly contested regions in Europe. In due course French dominance was challenged by an alliance presided over by Pope Julius II. When Milan became too dangerous Leonardo went to live with Melzi's parents for a time in 1513. He was again without a patron, and without the resources to put any of his grander schemes into practice. After some wanderings, he went, accompanied by Melzi and Salai, to Rome under the aegis of Giuliano de' Medici, brother of Pope Leo X, in the hope of securing commissions from the Vatican. Some artists were being paid lavishly, but Leonardo was by now getting old, and his health was failing. He never properly established himself in Rome. While he continued with his various researches, and was consulted about a number of schemes, he created no more great paintings.

In 1515 Louis XII died and was succeeded by François I. Eager for glory, François attacked Lombardy, and retook Milan. The small Italian states sought to accommodate themselves to revived French power. In the course of this, Leonardo made a mechanical lion as a gift for the French king. It walked a few paces, opened its mouth, and displayed to François a bunch of fleurs-de-lis. Since the lion was a symbol of Florence and the fleur-de-lis a symbol of France, this automaton was meant to be a message from Leonardo's Medici patron to François, reminding him that Florence, (where the Medici were now back in power), was a true friend to France.

Whatever the diplomatic effect of the lion, François asked Leonardo to go to France. Giuliano de' Medici died in March 1516. Again without a patron, Leonardo finally took François up on his offer, and left Italy for good late in 1516 or early in the following year. After the lean times he had been enduring, François proved a refreshingly attentive and generous master. He made over a manor near one of his own châteaux to Leonardo, and arranged handsome salaries for both Leonardo and Melzi.

Leonardo could no longer paint, since according to one account his right arm was paralysed; perhaps the witness meant his left arm (Leonardo was left-handed), or perhaps the paralysis was a symptom of an illness, for Leonardo's health was deteriorating. He had brought three paintings with him, however, including the *Mona Lisa*, and could continue to direct the work of his pupils, especially Melzi. He seems to have planned to arrange some of the voluminous material in his notebooks for publication, but possibly found it was too wide-ranging to be readily reduced into publishable form, for nothing came of it.

Vasari, who records in one edition of his *Lives of the Painters* that Leonardo was a heretic, tells of a deathbed repentance and Leonardo's return to the Church. This seems too much like conventional piety on Vasari's part to be wholly plausible. However, he also claimed that François arrived when Leonardo was about to die, and that Leonardo sat up in bed and sought to explain the nature of his illness. A final paroxysm interrupted him. François hastened forward, and Leonardo died in the king's arms. Whether true or not, it seems fitting that a man who had spent so long exploring the beauties and frailties of the human body, both as artist and as scientist, should persist in gathering evidence even about his own final illness.

He died on 2 May 1519. He was buried with full Catholic ceremony, as his will stipulated. Melzi, who had been with him to the end, supervised the winding up of his affairs. He took many of Leonardo's notebooks, and struggled to prepare them for the press, but in vain. After Melzi's death in 1570 the notebooks were scattered, and some of them were broken up by souvenir-seekers. Even today, when Leonardo's ambition to see them published has been realized, much is still missing. Many of his surviving paintings have been badly damaged. Strips have been cut from some, while insensitive restoration has removed some of the fine layers of paint in which Leonardo painstakingly accumulated such detail that those who saw them were astonished at their trueness to life. Leonardo remains elusive, but the legend of the universal genius, untrammelled by narrow specialism, and guided mainly by his own intuition, lives on.

In writing this short life of Leonardo I have been particularly indebted to Serge Bramly, *Leonardo: The Artist and the Man* (HarperCollins, 1992; Penguin Books, 1994) and to Irma A. Richter, Ed., *Selections from the Notebooks of Leonardo Da Vinci* (Oxford, 1952). They are excellent and complementary ways to learn more of Leonardo, and I recommend them warmly to any reader who wishes to do so.

FURTHER MINI SERIES INCLUDE

THEY DIED TOO YOUNG

Elvis
James Dean
Buddy Holly
Jimi Hendrix
Sid Vicious
Marc Bolan
Ayrton Senna
Marilyn Monroe
Jim Morrison

THEY DIED TOO YOUNG

Malcolm X
Kurt Cobain
River Phoenix
John Lennon
Glenn Miller
Isadora Duncan
Rudolph Valentino
Freddie Mercury
Bob Marley

FURTHER MINI SERIES
INCLUDE

HEROES OF THE WILD WEST

General Custer
Butch Cassidy and the Sundance Kid
Billy the Kid
Annie Oakley
Buffalo Bill
Geronimo
Wyatt Earp
Doc Holliday
Sitting Bull
Jesse James